Wolf Fables

Three fables, originally from Ancient Greece

Pie Corb

Illustrated
Ester Garcia
Inge-Marie J
Scott Plumbe

D1627996

The Wolf in .... othing 3
The Boy Who Cried 'Wolf!' 11
The Wolf and the Goat 25

Dear Reader,

These stories were told by a Greek slave called Aesop. He told over two hundred stories about animals. Each story is a fable, which means that it ends with a 'moral'. A moral explains what we can learn from the story.

I hope you enjoy them.

Pie Corbett

The Wolf in Sheep's Clothing

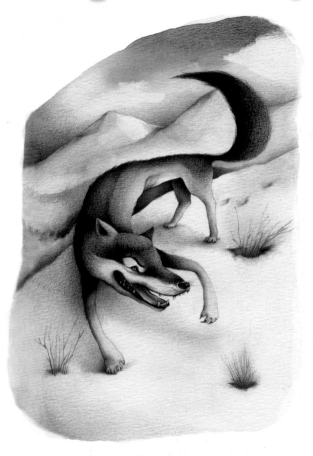

Once upon a time there was a sly old wolf. He was as skinny as a snake and hungry for meat.

One day, the wolf saw a flock of sheep on the hillside. There was snow on the ground and it was very cold. A shepherd was busy, feeding the sheep. He called them by their names and patted their backs.

The shepherd cared for his flock, but to the wolf they were nothing more than lamb chops.

Later that day, the wolf was out hunting on the snowy hillside. He found a sheepskin under a tree. An idea popped into the wolf's head. Perhaps he could dress up as a sheep and join the flock!

What a clever disguise! The shepherd
would never guess. The wolf could eat the
sheep one by one without anyone knowing.

The wolf felt his belly rumble!

In the evening, when the sun was setting, the wolf dressed himself in the sheepskin. The sheep were tired and cold. A few of them bleated when they saw him but all they wanted was the warmth of their pen.

The wolf snuggled down with the sheep.
There were more Sunday dinners here than in his
wildest dreams ... But his plan was not as
clever as he had hoped.

The shepherd wanted some
meat for his dinner. He went
down to the pen and chose
the thinnest looking sheep.

He killed it and took it home for his wife to roast. But they had quite a shock for it was not a sheep that he had killed. It was the wolf!

The shepherd thanked his lucky stars that he had killed the wolf and saved the rest of the flock.

Moral of the tale

Do not pretend to be something that you are not.

The Boy Who Cried 'Wolf!'

Everyone knows wolves are dangerous. They hunt in packs and it is not just lambs that they kill.

Everyone knows about the
wolf that tricked Little Red
Riding Hood ...

... and tried to eat the three little pigs.

Everyone knows that wolves are not to be trusted.

Once upon a time there was a young shepherd boy. His job was to look after the villagers' flock of sheep. Every morning, he took the flock to graze in the hills.

Every evening, he took them home again.

During the day there was not much to do. The sheep chewed the grass, the lambs bleated at each other and the ram slept.

The boy grew bored.

People say that the devil makes work for idle hands and this time he stirred up a whole cauldron of trouble! The boy decided to play a trick. He ran down the hill, shouting, 'Wolf! Wolf!'

At once, all the villagers came
out to protect their flock.

The boy hid behind a rock.

He laughed at the burly baker, the blacksmith, the red-faced butcher and the women as they ran up the hill.

They were shouting and waving their arms to chase off a wolf that did not exist.

In fact, the boy thought it was so funny that he did it again and again. Each time he pretended that the wolf had run away. It wasn't long before the villagers were fed up. They decided that the boy was tricking them.

Now tricks turn to trouble, as sure as snow melts in the sun. One day, a pack of wolves *did* come stalking out of the forest. They had eyes of fire and were so thin that their ribs showed through their fur.

The boy screamed, 'Wolf! Wolf!'
But no one came.

The blacksmith stopped with his hammer raised high. He listened to the boy's distant screams and just shook his head.

The women in the fields tut-tutted and carried on with their work.

The baker muttered, 'That shepherd boy, up to his tricks again!'

They all ignored the boy's screams.

Later that day, the shepherd boy returned to the village. There were no sheep with him, bleating. Just silence. The wolves had taken all the sheep. The shepherd boy had played the fool once too often and now he had made a fool of *himself.*

Moral of the tale

If you keep on lying then in the end no one will believe you – even if you are telling the truth.

The Wolf
and the Goat

Long ago, people believed that just one look from a wolf could make you blind! Of course, that was nonsense. But wolves are cunning and you need to be careful.

One day, a wolf fell into a water hole. He paddled up and down but the hole was too deep for him to climb out.

Soon, a thirsty goat came down to the water hole. Now, the wolf was cunning. He pretended to drink the water, even though it tasted stale. 'Mmmm, how sweet this water tastes,' he said.

At once, the goat leaped into the water hole to drink the tasty water. But how silly! Not only did the water taste like rotten eggs but now they were both trapped!

'Don't worry,' the wolf said. 'I have a plan. First, place your forefeet on the side of the hole. Then lower your head. I will run up your back and escape. Then, I'll be able to pull you out!'

Trusting the wolf, the goat carefully placed his forefeet on the side of the hole. Next, he lowered his head.

The wolf leaped onto his back and used the goat's horns to help him scramble to the top.

'Now, pull me up,' called the goat.
The wolf just turned and grinned back
at him.

'If you had as many brains in your head as you have hairs in your beard, you would have thought more carefully about what might happen.

'Did you not wonder if it was wise to jump into a hole with a wolf?'

Chuckling to himself, the wolf dashed away. Poor goat was left paddling up and down the water hole, wishing he had been wiser ... and wondering who might pass by next!

Moral of the tale

Always look and think before you leap.